— The —
MOST RELAXING SONGS
FOR PIANO SOLO

And So It Goes	2	The Music of Goodbye	
Annie's Song	4	My Heart Will Go On (Love Theme from 'Titanic')	60
Bella's Lullaby	6	New York State of Mind	64
Blowin' in the Wind	8	On Golden Pond	70
Brian's Song	10	Over the Rainbow	74
Cavatina	12	Perhaps Love	67
Cinema Paradiso	18	The Rose	76
(They Long to Be) Close to You	20	Somewhere in Time	78
Cristofori's Dream	22	(Theme from) A Summer Place	80
Dawn	28	Tara's Theme (My Own True Love)	83
Days of Wine And Roses	15	Tears in Heaven	86
Evergreen	32	Time After Time	88
Fields of Gold	36	A Time for Us (Love Theme)	90
Gabriel's Oboe	42	Unforgettable	92
Theme from Ice Castles (Through the Eyes of Love)	39	The Way We Were	94
Imagine	44	Where Do I Begin (Love Theme)	97
In a Sentimental Mood	47	The Wind Beneath My Wings	100
Longer	50	With You	110
Mia & Sebastian's Theme	53	Yesterday	104
Music Box Dancer	56	You've Got a Friend	106

ISBN 978-1-4950-9440-8

7777 W. BLUEMOUND RD. P.O. BOX 13819 MILWAUKEE, WI 53213

Visit Hal Leonard Online at
www.halleonard.com

AND SO IT GOES

Words and Music by
BILLY JOEL

Slow Ballad, with rubato

ANNIE'S SONG

Words and Music by
JOHN DENVER

BELLA'S LULLABY
from the Summit Entertainment film TWILIGHT

Composed by
CARTER BURWELL

BLOWIN' IN THE WIND

Words and Music by
BOB DYLAN

BRIAN'S SONG
Theme from the Screen Gems Television Production BRIAN'S SONG

Music by MICHEL LEGRAND

CAVATINA

from the Universal Pictures and EMI Films Presentation THE DEER HUNTER

By STANLEY MYERS

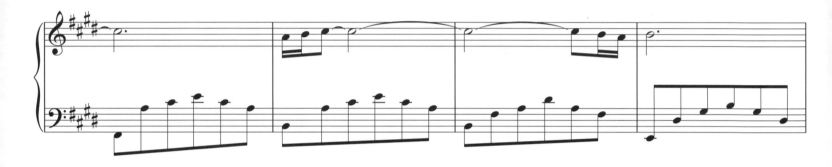

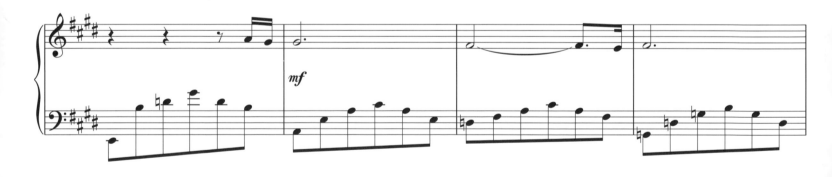

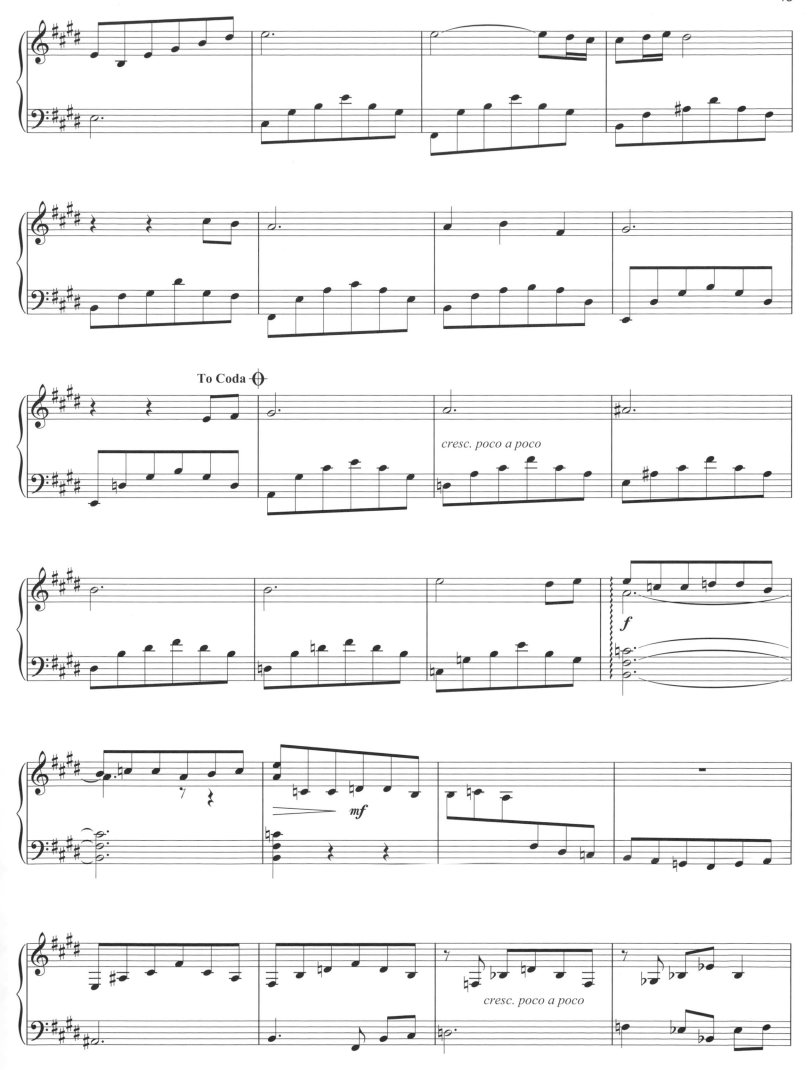

DAYS OF WINE AND ROSES

from DAYS OF WINE AND ROSES

Lyrics by JOHNNY MERCER
Music by HENRY MANCINI

CINEMA PARADISO
from CINEMA PARADISO

By ENNIO MORRICONE
and ANDREA MORRICONE

Simply, with feeling

(They Long to Be)
CLOSE TO YOU

Lyrics by HAL DAVID
Music by BURT BACHARACH

CRISTOFORI'S DREAM

By DAVID LANZ

DAWN
from PRIDE AND PREJUDICE

By DARIO MARIANELLI

Moderately fast, with motion

EVERGREEN
Love Theme from A STAR IS BORN

Words by PAUL WILLIAMS
Music by BARBRA STREISAND

FIELDS OF GOLD

Music and Lyrics by
STING

THEME FROM ICE CASTLES
(Through the Eyes of Love)
from ICE CASTLES

Music by MARVIN HAMLISCH
Lyrics by CAROLE BAYER SAGER

CODA

GABRIEL'S OBOE

from the Motion Picture THE MISSION

Music by ENNIO MORRICONE

Slowly, expressively

IMAGINE

Words and Music by
JOHN LENNON

IN A SENTIMENTAL MOOD

By DUKE ELLINGTON

LONGER

Words and Music by
DAN FOGELBERG

MIA & SEBASTIAN'S THEME
from LA LA LAND

Music by
JUSTIN HURWITZ

Moderately slow, expressively

With pedal

MUSIC BOX DANCER

Composed by
FRANK MILLS

THE MUSIC OF GOODBYE
from OUT OF AFRICA

Words and Music by JOHN BARRY,
ALAN BERGMAN and MARILYN BERGMAN

MY HEART WILL GO ON
(Love Theme from 'Titanic')
from the Paramount and Twentieth Century Fox Motion Picture TITANIC

Music by JAMES HORNER
Lyrics by WILL JENNINGS

NEW YORK STATE OF MIND

Words and Music by
BILLY JOEL

PERHAPS LOVE

Words and Music by
JOHN DENVER

ON GOLDEN POND
Main Theme from ON GOLDEN POND

Music by DAVE GRUSIN

OVER THE RAINBOW
from THE WIZARD OF OZ

Music by HAROLD ARLEN
Lyric by E.Y. "YIP" HARBURG

THE ROSE

from the Twentieth Century-Fox Motion Picture Release THE ROSE

Words and Music by
AMANDA McBROOM

SOMEWHERE IN TIME

from SOMEWHERE IN TIME

Music by JOHN BARRY

(Theme from)
A SUMMER PLACE
from A SUMMER PLACE

Words by MACK DISCANT
Music by MAX STEINER

TARA'S THEME
(My Own True Love)
from GONE WITH THE WIND

By MAX STEINER

TEARS IN HEAVEN

Words and Music by ERIC CLAPTON
and WILL JENNINGS

TIME AFTER TIME

from the Metro-Goldwyn-Mayer Picture IT HAPPENED IN BROOKLYN

Words by SAMMY CAHN
Music by JULE STYNE

A TIME FOR US
(Love Theme)
from the Paramount Picture ROMEO AND JULIET

Words by LARRY KUSIK and EDDIE SNYDER
Music by NINO ROTA

UNFORGETTABLE

Words and Music by
IRVING GORDON

THE WAY WE WERE

from the Motion Picture THE WAY WE WERE

Words by ALAN and MARILYN BERGMAN
Music by MARVIN HAMLISCH

Rubato, expressively

Slowly, steadily

Bring out melody

WHERE DO I BEGIN
(Love Theme)
Theme from the Paramount Picture LOVE STORY

Words by CARL SIGMAN
Music by FRANCIS LAI

THE WIND BENEATH MY WINGS

from the Original Motion Picture BEACHES

Words and Music by LARRY HENLEY
and JEFF SILBAR

Flowing slowly, in 2

YESTERDAY

Words and Music by JOHN LENNON
and PAUL McCARTNEY

YOU'VE GOT A FRIEND

Words and Music by
CAROLE KING

WITH YOU
from PIPPIN

Words and Music by
STEPHEN SCHWARTZ